A Character Building Book™

Learning About Compassion from the Life of

Florence Nightingale

Kiki Mosher

The Rosen Publishing Group's
PowerKids Press™
New York

Published in 1996 by The Rosen Publishing Group, Inc.
29 East 21st Street, New York, NY 10010

First Edition

Book design: Erin McKenna

Photo credits: Cover © Archive Photos; pp. 19, 20 © The Bettmann Archive; all other photos © Corbis-Bettmann.

Mosher, Kiki.
    Learning about compassion from the life of Florence Nightingale / by Kiki Mosher.
        p.   cm. — (A Character building book)
    Includes index.
    Summary: A brief biography of the woman whose concern for others led her to become a pioneer in the field of nursing.
    ISBN 0-8239-2423-8
    1. Nightingale, Florence, 1820–1910—Juvenile literature. 2. Nurses—England—Biography—Juvenile literature. 3. Caring—Juvenile literature. [1. Nightingale, Florence, 1820–1910. 2. Nurses. 3. Women—Biography. 4. Caring.] I. Title. II. Series.
RT37.N5M67 1996
610.73'092—dc20
                                                    96-3511
                                                  CIP
                                                    AC

Table of Contents

Feeling Compassion

Florence Nightingale was born in Florence, Italy, more than 100 years ago. She grew up in England. From the time she was a little girl, Florence felt **sympathy** (SIM-path-ee) and **compassion** (kum-PASH-un) for people who suffered. She saw their pain and wanted to help them. She was also very smart.

◀ *Florence grew up feeling compassion for those who suffered.*

Challenging Women's Roles

When Florence was young, girls were taught that they should be quiet and pretty. Young women were expected to get married and have children. They were not encouraged to work outside the home. Florence, the daughter of wealthy parents, decided that she wanted to do something different. Like many girls at that time, Florence wasn't allowed to go to school. So she began reading in her father's library. She learned many things. She **dared** (DAYRD) to be different.

Florence educated herself by reading books from her father's library. ▶

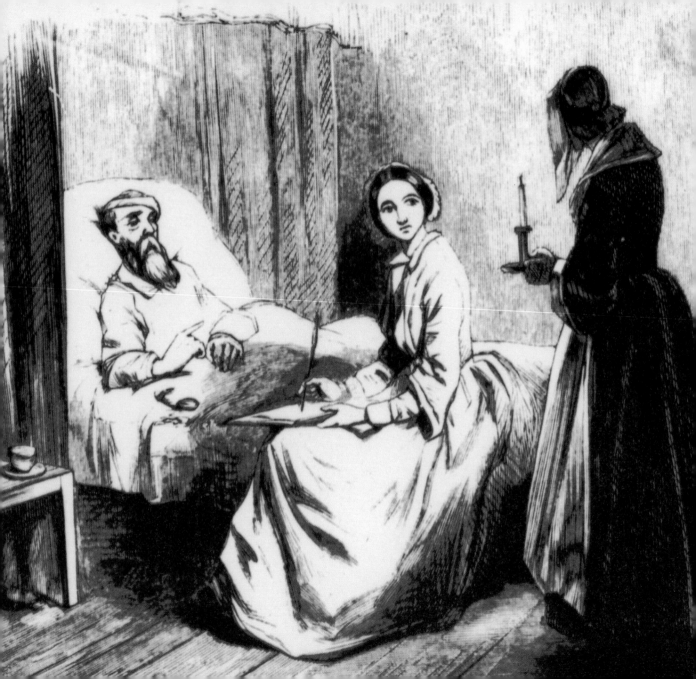

Caring for Others

Florence liked studying, but she wanted to help others. She persuaded her parents to let her visit sick people. At first she brought them food and kept them company. Then she began to pay more attention to their health. She made sure they were clean and comfortable. She realized that this made a difference and improved their health.

◀ *Florence showed her compassion by visiting and caring for people who were sick.*

Compassion in the Hospital

When she was about 30 years old, Florence realized that she wanted to become a nurse and work in a **hospital** (HOS-pih-tul). Her parents didn't like that idea at all. In those days, it was considered unladylike to be a nurse. The only patients in hospitals were poor people. Hospitals were crowded, dirty, smelly places full of disease. Hospitals spread more illnesses than they cured. People often became more sick or died because of the conditions in hospitals. But Florence knew she could make things better.

Florence realized that keeping sick and hurt people clean helped them get well. ▶

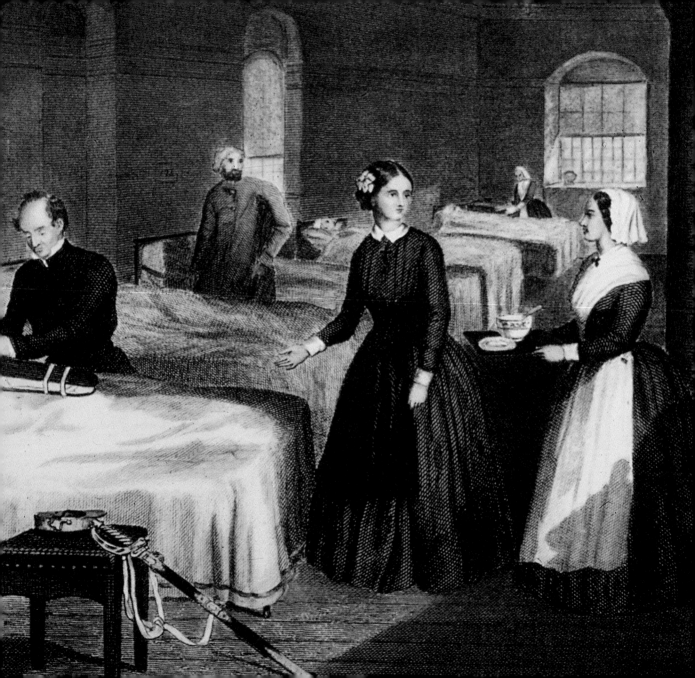

Learning to Be a Nurse

Florence spent a few months **volunteering** (vol-un-TEER-ing) in hospitals in Germany and France. There she learned basic nursing skills. Soon after, Florence became the head nurse in a hospital in London. She made sure the hospital was cleaned regularly. She kept beds, sheets, clothes, and equipment clean. This helped keep disease from spreading around the hospital. People began to get well faster because of her actions. Florence was quiet, strong, gentle, and wise. Other nurses began to follow her example.

◀ *Many nurses followed Florence's example in caring for the patients.*

The Crimean War

In 1853, Russia tried to take land from Turkey. England and France joined Turkey in fighting Russia. This was the beginning of the **Crimean War** (cry-ME-an WOR). Battles were violent and bloody. There was no one to take care of the hurt soldiers. Many died.

The man who sent British soldiers to fight was named Sidney Herbert. He was worried about his soldiers. He knew about and admired Florence's work with the sick. He asked her to help.

Many soldiers were hurt or killed in the Crimean War. ▶

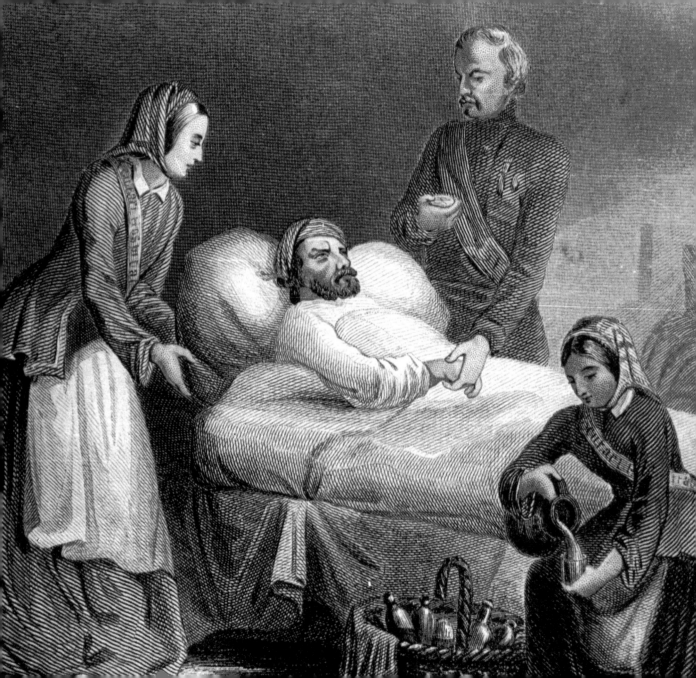

Hard Work

Florence organized a team of nurses to travel to Turkey. They helped the sick and hurt soldiers. The conditions there were terrible. There was no hospital, very little water, and no medical equipment. Wounded soldiers were left unbathed, without food or clean clothing. More hurt soldiers arrived every day. The first thing Florence did was clean and paint the building. She bought food, medicine, sheets, and clothes. She organized a kitchen and laundry. The soldiers improved under her kind yet firm command. She and her nurses saved many lives.

◀ *Florence and her nurses made sure that the injured soldiers were bathed and fed regularly.*

The Lady with the Lamp

Florence often worked 20 hours a day. She tried to make life better for the soldiers in the hospital. She cooked for them, bathed them, talked to them, and comforted them. She believed that sick or hurt people should be cared for day and night. Every night, carrying her lantern, she went from bed to bed to make sure each soldier was doing well. They began to call her the "Lady with the Lamp."

Florence's constant care earned her the nickname the "Lady with the Lamp." ▶

A National Heroine

Florence returned to London after the war. All of England knew about the woman who helped save the lives of thousands of soldiers. Florence was a national **heroine** (HEH-roh-in).

Florence continued to help the sick and the poor. She wrote many books about nursing, the way hospitals work, and the need to keep hospitals clean and free from germs. During the American Civil War and other wars that followed, many soldiers benefited from the changes Florence had made to health care during the Crimean War.

◀ *Florence helped improve the way sick people were cared for. She is a heroine.*

Nightingale Nurses

Sidney Herbert wanted to show how much he appreciated what Florence had done and how many people she had helped. He helped her open the Nightingale Training School in London. There, students, called "Nightingale nurses," were trained in nursing. Florence set many of the standards of health, cleanliness, and compassion that nursing still follows today.

At the end of her nursing career Florence wrote, "To be a good nurse, one has to be a good person."

Florence lived to be 90 years old.

Glossary

compassion (kum-PASH-un) A feeling of strongly wanting to help others.

Crimean War (cry-ME-an WOR) War fought by England, France, Turkey on one side, and Russia on the other. It lasted from 1853 to 1856.

dare (DAYR) Take a risk.

heroine (HEH-roh-in) A girl or woman to whom other people look up.

hospital (HOS-pih-tul) Place where doctors and nurses take care of sick and hurt people.

sympathy (SIM-path-ee) The ability to share a feeling.

volunteer (vol-un-TEER) To work without pay.

23

Index